masquerade

masquerade

cyrus parker

Andrews McMeel
PUBLISHING®

also by cyrus parker

poetry

DROPKICKromance

anthologized works

"Where the Sea Meets the Sky"
featured in
[Dis]Connected: Poems & Stories of Connection and Otherwise

for those who have yet to figure out
just who it is they are:

you'll get there.
one day, you'll get there.

content warning

masquerade contains sensitive material relating
to the following topics:

abandonment, alcohol use, death, gender dysphoria,
harassment, intimate partner abuse, and potentially more.

please remember to practice self-care before,
during, and after reading.

contents

From childhood's hour I have not been
As others were—I have not seen
As others saw—I could not bring
My passions from a common spring—

— "Alone," Edgar Allan Poe

this is it.

this is where the truth comes out.
this is where every road converges.
this is where the masks finally come off.
this is the masquerade.

innocence

whatever happened to the one
whose hands could take pencil to paper
and turn imagination into reality?
whose feet could walk out the backyard door
and into another world?
the one with eyes ready to swallow the sky whole
and a heart ambitious enough to do it?

whatever happened to the one
who raced from dawn 'til dusk,
waving in the wind on wings of wax
to wrap their fingertips around the sun,
yet cowered from the glow of streetlights?
the one who decided even the sun wasn't enough
and pocketed entire galaxies instead?

whatever happened to the one
whose dreams were so grand
the universe itself had to expand
to keep up the pace?
the one who refused to be contained
and became a universe themself?
the one you're thinking about right now?

skull kid

childhood is the time
when one reaches
toward the sky
and grows into the person
they were meant to be,
but

my childhood was the time
when i reached
toward fictional faces
and buried my roots
within a flawless
facade.

my childhood was the time
when i rejected
my own growth to mirror
the growth of others because
i wasn't sure who i was
supposed to be.

rest in pieces

i remember slamming pogs
in the basement and mighty
morphin' power rangers figures.
i remember birthday parties
at major magic's and weekend
sleepovers. i remember tapping
him on the shoulder and calling
his name as he walked away,
and how not one word followed
the sudden and unexpected
death of our friendship.
major magic and his animatronic,
anthropomorphic friends
followed a similar fate.
their motions became forced
and jerky, like the possessed
during an exorcism; and then,
one day, their mechanical mouths
mimed the beatles' happy birthday song
for the last time, and the doors to that
magical-kingdom-turned-ghost-town
were locked and bolted shut,
a time capsule to once upon a time.

misplaced

i was a piece of a puzzle
lost in the box of another.
no matter where you tried to put me,
which way you tried to turn me,
there wasn't a place for me in the big
picture, and i got tired of trying to fit
into places i didn't belong.

the masked magician

beware of those who take the magic
from their palms and place it in yours,
for as soon as you learn how to make
it your own, they'll do whatever it takes
to credit themselves for what now flows
through every fiber of your being.

stained glass mirror

you want so desperately
to please everybody,
so you chip off a piece
of all those you meet
and stick them together,
a mosaic of everything
you think
they could ever want you to be—
but when you break yourself down
into such tiny, little pieces,
there's never quite enough
of any one thing
to keep them satisfied.

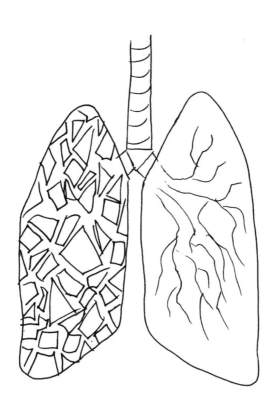

misconception

most think a chameleon changes
its skin to fit in with its surroundings,

but it's more of a socializing mechanism,
a way to communicate with others.

in this way, i am like the chameleon—
i've worn masks in so many colors,

i've said things i never should have said,
i've done things i never should have done,

become someone i never should have become.

normalize

a child stands in front of a mirror,
dissecting their own reflection
with scalpel-like precision.

why was i born like this?
why can't i change what i was given?
why don't i get a say in who i am?

the mirror doesn't answer, doesn't offer any
insight into the truth, because there is no
magic here, just a man-made construct.

ajar

i am a door,
a door that is always open,
a door with no welcome mat
that people walk in
and walk out of
as they please,
leaving only their
muddy footprints behind.

i am a door,
a door that is always closed,
a door with no locks
that people walk in
and walk out of
as they please,
never leaving
anything behind.

death's-head

when this caterpillar emerged from its cocoon,
it didn't have the prismatic wings of a butterfly
but ones as black as night, marked in the center
with a skull-shaped warning: *don't get too close.*

smokey eye

eyeliner as defiance.
eyeliner as a statement,
a declaration, a *fuck you*
to a society that shames
people for expressing
themselves the way they
feel the most at home,
the same society that labels
everything from toys to
toothbrushes "boy" and "girl"
rather than letting individuals
cultivate their own identities.

eyeliner as a call to arms.
eyeliner as a weapon,
a raised fist, a shield
from judgmental expressions
and microaggressions
disguised as questions,
from the insults and slurs
shot out of car windows
like bullets in a drive-by
because i dare exist
in a way they don't
and refuse to understand.

bigger

if they tell you to change who you are,
be yourself but even louder.

fixer-upper

self-confidence is built in layers,
the same way a house begins

with bare bones before becoming a home;
and just as each house has its own layout,

there isn't only one set of blueprints,
one *right* way to build self-confidence.

sometimes it starts from the inside out
as one learns to love themselves, and

sometimes it starts from the outside in
as one projects the person they hope to be.

sometimes, you have to tear everything
down and start over from the ground up.

rebirth

they told me
the best characters
are born
when you turn yourself
up to 100

so i cranked myself
up to 1,000
ripped the dial off
and smashed it to pieces
underneath my boot.

kayfabe:

/ˈkāˌfāb/
noun

the art of pretending to be someone you're not
until you lose sight of who it was you were.

spoiler alert: the monster isn't actually the monster

from the very second
i stepped through the curtain,
i began my experiment.
like a modern-day frankenstein,
i sought out to create
a perfect human.
i'd tweak my behavior
my mannerisms
the way i'd talk
even the way i'd walk.
if there was no response,
i'd nix it.
if there was,
i'd keep it,
and before long
i had them in
the palm of my hands.
if i wanted them to laugh,
they laughed.
if i wanted them to cry,
they cried.
if i wanted them to love me,
they loved me.

oh, how they loved me.

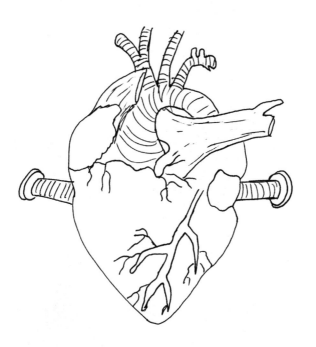

the king of games

the jester made himself a crown
and called himself a king,
and that made all the difference.

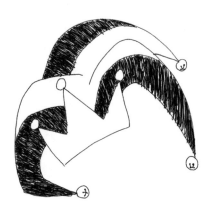

who am i?
after emily dickinson

i am nobody,
      and i am somebody,
      you see.
one day,
      the worm slowly
      snaking on the
      sidewalk, and
      the next, the
      circling crow.

i am somebody
      and i am nobody,
      you see.
nobody wants
      to be somebody,
      but somebody
      becomes nobody,
      despite what
      they believe.

daze of the week

sunday, i walk through the velvet curtain in a sequined vest into an arena filled with people chanting my name.

monday, i walk through the stockroom doors in a cotton vest into a store filled with people paging my clock number.

tuesday, a customer asks me if i'm that wrestler they saw at the show last weekend. i rip my name badge off and say yes.

wednesday, i have the day off, so i spend it studying and honing my craft.

thursday, the new schedule is finally posted.

friday, i tell them they scheduled me while i'm at my "other job." they tell me it's not their problem.

saturday, they tell me to choose between making a living or chasing a dream. i tell them i will not be in tomorrow.

linked

imagine wearing a mask for so long
that the skin beneath learns its shape
and begins tracing its edges, blurring
the lines between person and persona.

imagine the searing realization when
you try tearing it off for the first time,
unaware of just how much of your life
you have allowed this act to become.

imagine the patience and the precision
needed to delicately sever the bond
and pull the skin away from the mask
to remove the facade from the flesh.

imagine the confusion when you see
yourself for the first time without it,
and the face looking back at you is one
you no longer recognize as your own.

murder

it's a bit maddening, you know, to feel more at home pretending to be someone else than you do being yourself. you walk a little taller, hold your head up a little higher, speak a little louder, command attention just by being present. it's like every cell in your body forgets its original function and begins specializing in mass producing self-confidence. and it's intoxicating, so much so that you start doing whatever you can to keep it going. want becomes need and need becomes second nature, and you feel untouchable. but you're not. reality has a way of circling over you until you're at your most vulnerable before swooping down and tearing you apart layer by layer—skin, muscle, organ—until you're stripped down to the bone and left with the task of rebuilding yourself with only a memory to guide you.

the collector

every time i peel back another layer, every time i feel like i've finally gotten to the very core of who i am, i find that i've still done little more than scratch the surface. so i peel, and i peel, and i peel, and i peel, and i peel, and i begin wondering if i even really exist or if i'm just a collection of everything i'd hoped to be but never became.

a brief conversation with my reflection

i don't know how to be without you.

you'll never truly be without me.

how can that be possible?

you made me from a part
of you, remember?

i remember.

even when you thought
you were somebody else,
you were always still
you.

graverobber

my mouth has become a cemetery,
lined with the headstones of every word

that has died on my tongue
while escaping my spiderweb-throat.

i've tried digging up the corpses,
piecing their bones back together

and spitting out their skeletons, but
i kept choking on the graveyard dirt,

so i had a few drinks to make it easier.
the first to wash down the soil,

the second to burn away the threads,
and the third to find the courage

to wrap my lips around the words
that would set me free from the tomb

i've been trapped inside
from the moment i was conceived.

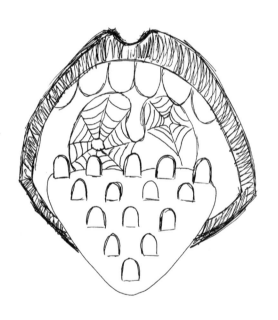

ruination

every time i try to make sense
of the disconnect between who i am
on the inside
versus
who i am on the outside,
i am interrupted
by a voice
that only repeats the same line:

you are broken.
you are broken.
you are broken.

and that is all it takes
to send me back within myself,
to make me deny every single question
i've ever been bold enough
to ask out loud.
maybe i am broken,
but nobody
will ever know
how broken i am.

the alchemy of me

i think back to the version of me
who figured out how to transmute
self-doubt into self-confidence

and wonder if he'd be proud
of the mess i have become—
the person who struggles

to make eye contact
with their own reflection;
the one who craves acceptance

but still keeps the world
at arm's length. every time
i empty another bottle

of whiskey into my glass,
i see him shaking his head
because when his demons came,

he'd face them one-on-one
and leave them tapping in submission.
it's true that i've figured out

something about myself
that even he couldn't
piece together,

but is that enough?
am i enough?
will i ever learn

how to turn water
into wine?
lead into gold?

liquid truth

when inhibitions are lowered,
the truth often comes pouring out.
the things i've felt forced to hide
step into the light, and it burns
to hear those words spilling so loosely
from my lips, like a shot glass running
over. the aftertaste lingers for days,
and in it i find words i never knew,
ones that explain what i thought
was a defect in my manufacturing.
no, i work just fine, and for the first
time i'm learning i am not alone.

binary breaker

i dream of deconstruction, breaking
myself down to the cellular level
analyzing my genetic material
tinkering with my chromosomes
following my own set of blueprints.

i dream of reconstruction, building
myself back up to the human form
watching myself become the person
on the outside that has been screaming
on the inside, hoping anyone would hear.

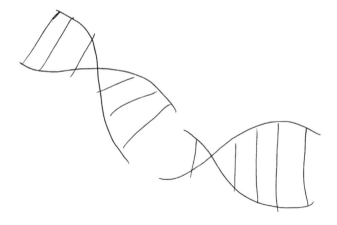

hate/hate relationship

some days, i hate my body for what it is.
other days, i hate my body for what it isn't.

october 25, 2016

i have been alive for twenty-nine years,
and i still don't know what that means.

dysphoria i

sometimes
i look at others
and wonder
if i'd be more
comfortable in my
skin if i wore
theirs.

dysphoria ii

would you
mind if i sliced
you open
and stepped inside
your body for a while?
mine has become
unbearable.

october 24, 2017

i don't know how much longer
i can stay in a body
that's never felt like home;
in a mind that knows the problem
but hasn't the slightest idea
how to fix it;
a life where a glass of whiskey
holds more truth
than my own honest heart
ever will.

lost & found

where does the confidence go when it's lost?
does it cease to be, or does it find a new host?
does it watch from afar as i struggle to keep
my head above water, when my own mind
is the one hell-bent on trying to pull me under?

choke

my name doesn't fit quite
right these days, like a shirt
whose collar wraps around
the neck a little too tightly.

not so tight that it stops my
breath but just enough to
leave me tugging at it every
time it touches my throat.

you are what you fear

when i was younger,
i feared the dark, not knowing
what monsters hid in the shadows,

but now i find comfort
in the late hours, the peace,
the silence,

and sometimes i wonder if i've
now become the very thing
i once feared.

whiskey nights

it's 4:31 in the morning, and i'm finally sobering up.
my eyelids are growing heavy as sleep calls for me, but
she is calling louder.

new york

the city doesn't care.
it pays no mind and
casts no judgment.

it's here, in this endless
sea of faces, where i feel
most comfortable being me.

start → power →
shut down

the older i get
the harder it is to relate
to those around me.

i walk the crowded streets,
cram myself into the jam-packed subway car,
sit in a room full of like-minded individuals,

and my skin begins to crawl,
my mind plots out escape routes,
and i retreat into myself when it all becomes too much.

my relationships are like phones
that only play the off-the-hook sound,
a wi-fi connection without a modem.

when my laptop reads "network error,"
there are at least a dozen ways
to troubleshoot the problem.

when i read "network error,"
there are zero ways
to troubleshoot me.

dawn of the final day

time is a two-faced mistress
in the way she both heals
things and destroys them.

i consider my once-broken
heart, healed by the methodical
ticking of the clock's hands.

i consider my soul growing
bitter like a pot of coffee left out
on the kitchen table too long.

i consider the lessons both
taught and later forgotten as
our minds transform with age.

i consider all the people that
have come and gone in my life
and wonder who still thinks of me.

resentment is the thing with fangs i

i've learned
to hold my grudges
much too closely.
i feel their teeth
scraping against my skin,
threatening to tear me
limb from limb
should i slip up
and lose control.

resentment is the thing with fangs ii

i've learned
to train my grudges
far too viciously.
i see their teeth
bare as they snarl,
threatening to tear them
limb from limb
should they ever come back
looking for my kindness.

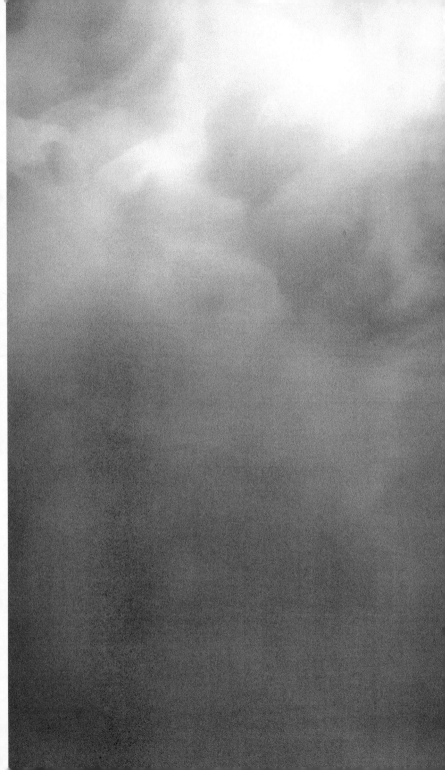

ii

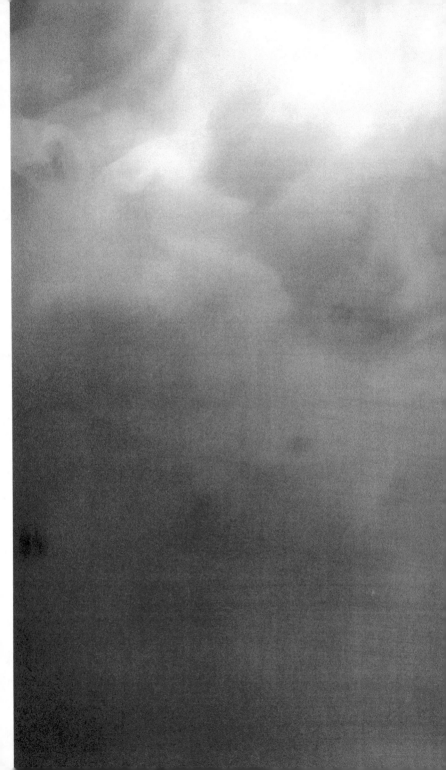

what's in a name?

my name was passed down to me
from my father and to him
from his father. i am the third
of this namesake, and i will be
the last. the first has passed on,
and the second remains a shell
of the man he used to be.
my name carries the weight
of every mistake they've made,
their failed attempts at decency.
my name is not my name but
the name of someone i once was.
my name is a reminder that
there are no good men left.

landslide

i remember that day like it was yesterday.
the text message as i punched out of work,
the way the air was sucked out of my lungs
when i stepped into what was once a home.
the broken hearts of your broken family.
the helplessness that gave way to rage.
the avalanche you left in your wake as you
ran away from the only life you'd known
because you were too much of a coward
to face the consequences of your actions.
the way you took everything, leaving us
without so much as a shovel to dig
ourselves back out of the wreckage.

12 things my father missed out on after he left:

1. my last day home
2. meeting the love of my life
3. my first day of college
4. my engagement
5. my wedding
6. my first apartment
7. my first book
8. my college graduation
9. my first house
10. six years of birthdays (and counting)
11. my second book
12. my respect

fault lines

i kept asking myself if there was something i could've done to change the outcome, said something to make you stay. that's how it always goes when someone leaves, though, isn't it? you think about every interaction you've had with them and try to pinpoint the exact moment in time that set everything into motion, like if you had handled things just a little differently, then maybe, just maybe, everything would be okay—they would still be here and you wouldn't have this guilt filling the hole their absence left inside of you. but sometimes there's nothing that could've changed what happened. sometimes, a person's place in your life is meant to be temporary. sometimes, it's okay to put the blame on them, where it belongs, rather than on yourself.

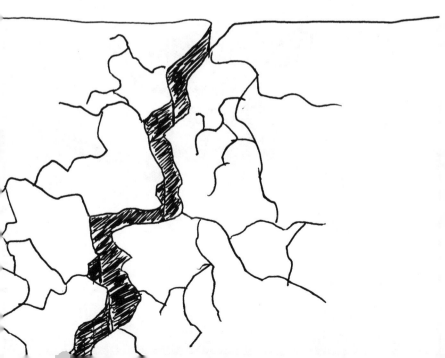

impractical magic

i may have become quite the escape artist,
but you mastered the disappearing act.

last rites

it's a strange thing to see your name in the title

of an obituary because you happen to share

a name with your now-deceased grandfather.

it's a strange thing to see your name in the body

of an obituary as one who has survived the dead

when you became the family's ghost

long before he ever passed away.

eulogy

i skipped the funeral.
we all knew it was for the best
even if excommunication is easier
than admitting that harsh truth.
how could i be expected to mourn
the man who watched us grovel
at his feet for help while
hiding the fact that he knew
all about what you had done to us?
how could i be expected
to come face-to-face with you
for the first time in two years
with an audience of people
who'd already taken your side
even though you were
the one who fucked up?
how could i be expected
to coexist with family
who no longer looked
at me as one of them?

the severed limb
of the family tree

no more forced smiles.
no more *you should come*
visit more oftens or
remember the times.
no more late birthday cards
or awkward gift exchanges.
no more feigned interest
in each other's lives.
two families who couldn't
be more different got together
in silent understanding
and sawed off the branch
that joined them,
leaving it to rot while
carrying on as if it never
existed in the first place.

spit

i have not seen you
in six years, but when
i look at pictures of myself,
when i brush my teeth
in the morning and catch
my reflection from the wrong
angle, your face meets mine
your eyes
your nose
your jaw
my mouth
my mouth
my mouth
i spit into the sink
i gargle mouthwash
i spit into the sink again
i run the water
and i rinse your name
right down the drain

your name is NOT
my name your
NAME is not my
NAME your
name is NOT
MY NAME

conflicted

thinking about you
is like walking a tightrope.
i try to keep the balance
between love and hate
because i believe in nothing
if not nuance,
and while i love the genuinely good
father i had for the first twenty-five
years of my life, i cannot stomach
the man who decided
to become nothing
more than a memory
for the last six.

when your ex slides into your
dms to confront you about
your poetry:

you talk to me like not a moment
has passed between then and now,
but the person you used to know
died a long time ago.

the cleansing

every poet has that one
person they swear they'll
never write about again,
and your ghost refuses
to stop haunting my fingertips.
i wrote half a book of poetry
about you, and it was supposed
to be a eulogy, an exorcism,
but instead i seemed to have
disturbed the grounds.
i've built a castle of quartz
and circled it in salt,
but still you manage
to find a way through the cracks.

recovery

when i yelled and screamed,
you pretended not to hear;
but when i learned to keep quiet,
you refused to break the silence.
now that i've found my voice,

you want to put out its fire
before you get burned.
i understand the instinct
of self-preservation,
but i also understand the poison

of unspoken words—
the way the mind rots
from the inside out.
the way the heart ices over
from the outside in.

masquerade

the way a mortal
becomes a monster.
and i have done too many monstrous
things, accumulated too many regrets,
given in to too many vices

to erase all the mistakes i've made
to forget who i used to be
to let myself once again become
the person who was frightened by
the movement of their own shadow.

i am become

do not for a second think
that i didn't catch the spite
dripping from your words
when you told me
you understand
that i have

become a writer.
you yourself are a writer,
and every writer knows
how one's choice of words
can alter the entire meaning
of the message they're trying to convey.

become a writer,
like i'm simply trying out
a new look because it's
the latest style
and not because it's how i feel
most comfortable.

become a writer,
like i didn't spend seven years
filling page after page of journal entries,
screaming into a void because i
didn't have anyone to talk to
about the train wreck that was us.

become a writer,
like i wasn't filling notebooks
and word documents with stories
where i wrote myself
into my favorite fictional worlds
because i needed an escape from this one.

become a writer,
like i didn't spend five years
developing a character, writing my dialogue,
carefully sculpting the facade
whose mind i would retreat inside
when i could no longer stay in mine.

become a writer,
like i didn't spend three years
burying myself in debt
honing my craft
and earning a degree
doing *this*.

become a writer?
darling, i've *always*
been one—
i'm just not telling
the story
you want to read.

cataclysm

we were like two planets, free from our orbits, hurtling toward one another for years. the inevitable impact was cataclysmic, and neither one of us made it out in one piece. i tend to think you made it out a little more whole than i, but perhaps i am a bit biased. still, we promised each other more than forever—we even made up our own word for whatever that meant. i think in a fucked up kind of way that promise still holds true, because the surface of my being has been forever altered by the intersection of our paths, and that impact will stay with me for as long as my presence exists in this world. when i am but ashes, they will be missing the bits of me that you took. when they read my poetry, they'll read the words of the person you helped shape me into.

ineffectual poetics

you say you want us to talk this out,
but i have nothing left to say
that hasn't already been said.
i know these poems are addressed *to* you,
but that doesn't mean they're *for* you
you
YOU
called the act
of me dissecting my own corpse
and performing the autopsy
on my rotting remains
on paper, in verse,
"ineffectual poetics."

and i'm not sure if i should be relieved
that you called it *poetry*
when there is a war raging
against the poets
who dare set the rule book aside
and write their truths their way

or if i should be sad
that you'll never truly understand
how cathartic this is for me
because it's ineffectual
in giving you whatever it is
you're still hoping to find in me.

masquerade

those seven years changed the both of us,
and the years that followed even more so.
you discovered the path leading
to your own personal peace,
and for that, i am happy,
but i still have a long way to go
before i find mine.
so i'll continue writing
until i finally resemble "fine,"
because while you might not be the person
i wrote those poems about any longer,
i am who i am today
because of her,
and just because you've burned the body
and let the wind carry her away
doesn't mean
her spirit
has
stopped

lingering.

divination

i'm beginning to realize
that it isn't your ghost
i should be warding off,
because when i asked
the spirit board to reveal
the name of the one
haunting me,
it didn't spell your name,
it spelled mine.

little blue book of poems

i'm sorry if it came off like our entire relationship was a black hole that devoured every bit of light in both of our lives. there were good moments that i didn't write into our story, like the time you hopped in a car and drove six hours to get to my back doorstep and surprise me with a handful of days together. the truth is, my memory isn't the greatest, and i couldn't remember if that happened on valentine's day or if i was confusing it with the other valentine's day that ended in a goodbye. i promised myself i would never write a single word that wasn't honest, so it's a shame that the only moments that seem to stick are the ones i'd rather forget.

closure i

if you want me to stop writing about you, stop
giving me something to write about.

closure ii

i promise to never again let your name reach my fingers,
if you promise to never speak mine.

closure iii

amanda once wrote the line "poetry will not make you immortal," and i pray she's right.

laced with love

she is the only one who can say my name
and put out fires rather than start them.

to us

she sips rosé and i sip whiskey,
and i can't help but think about
how perfectly that describes us:
her, a slow, sweet burn, and me,
a little too much all at once.

the countdown

two weeks—
that's when it
finally hit me.
two weeks until
you walk down
the aisle at our
favorite place,
in front of our
favorite people.
two weeks until
we take each
other by the hand,
and you and i
become one.

october 13, 2017

she walked out from beneath the canopy
with autumn wrapped around her body
and twilight courting night in her hair.
the sun, moon, and stars trailed behind,
taking in the light only she could give.

no roots

home is a five-hour car ride through winding roads as the sun first peeks over the hilltops. home is airports, train stations, taxis, and hotel rooms. home is a bench beside a lake and a bridge spanning a river. home is the bookstores, coffee shops, and every single aisle in target. home is anywhere i have left my footprints beside yours.

writer's block

even on my days off,
i can't seem to rest.
sleep is wasted time,
and there isn't much time
in this life to waste,
so i creep out of bed at seven thirty—
quietly, as not to wake my wife,
because she deserves the sleep i cannot entertain.
i feed our cat, and she lies next to me
as i sit at the kitchen table
with my laptop and a cup of coffee.
my fingers hover over the keys,
and i expect the words to
pour out like syrup,
thick and sweet and raw,
but the words don't come.
my fingers don't press the keys
that don't log the letters
that i don't shape into the words
that i don't string into the lines
of poetry that i don't write.
there isn't much time
in this life to waste,
and yet it's all i seem
to know how to do.

imposter syndrome

"what happens if i fail?"
"that's an impossibility."
"how can you be so sure?"
"because you are poetry."

spell tag

i used to believe that my ghosts
would follow me to the grave,
and maybe they will, but i know
they don't come for me as often
as they used to because they can't
thrive in the light; and with you near,
i've all but forgotten what the dark
looks like.

ace of hearts

i could fall 1,001 times
and still consider myself
the luckiest person in the
universe, because i know
every single time i do,
it'll be your hands reaching
for mine, helping me back
to my feet.

the truth within the truth

some say you are whole
without another's soul,
and i used to disagree
because i was certain
that we were two halves
to one whole; but i see now
that maybe we're not
but instead two souls
designed to complement
one another so well that
seeing each other from afar
is like looking into a mirror
and recognizing your own
reflection, and getting up close
is noticing all the little differences
that make you who you are
and me who i am.

sun, rain & soil

she says flowers grow
wherever my fingertips graze,
but every bud bursting from beneath
the surface is because she dared
blossom despite those who thought
her petals were theirs for the picking.

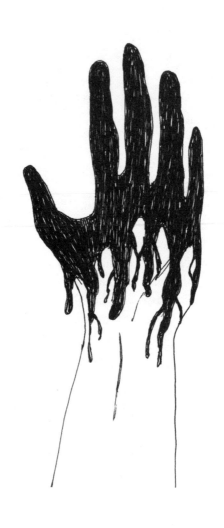

creation vs. destruction

i have a problem with constantly trying to be something i'm not. i write poems and draw pictures because i want to bring something beautiful into this world, but my hands only know destruction. i no longer trust myself with the things i care about most because i am afraid my fingerprints will leave them marked. i no longer trust myself to hold her hand because i am afraid my hands will teach her hands their language.

5:30 a.m.

some envy the mug
that touches your lips
in the early morning,
but i envy the first sip
of coffee that wraps
around your soul like a hug
and helps you get through
even the toughest of days.

the only one

with you, there is no pretending.
you see me like nobody sees me.
you know me like nobody knows me.
you accept me like nobody accepts me.

water witch

it's a rainy september morning,
and autumn brushes her lips gently
against our skin for the first time

this year, and it's like every poem
i've ever written about us—you
and me sitting in our favorite café,

sipping on cups of pumpkin spice,
legs tangled beneath the table, but now,
in the moments between stanzas,

i absentmindedly reach for the ring
you slid onto my finger last october.
now, there is an apartment for us

to return to, but only for another month
because soon we'll be packing up
everything we've collected over the years

and moving it into a house of our very own,
with a window perch for our cat and a tiny
little deck in the back for drinking coffee

and watching the yellows, reds, and oranges
dance in the wind in celebration of the new
life we've built for ourselves.

iii

phases

sometimes i feel as if
the moon shines for me
and me alone.
i look up and marvel
at the way she changes
her masks,
wearing a new face
every single night
but remaining unmistakably
herself.
i too
have worn many masks,
and i'm only now
beginning to understand
that at my very core
i've always been the same.

better late than never

the problem with me has always been that i waste too much time looking for the validation of others, when the only validation i needed was my own. i might not be all the way there yet, but one day, i will be. and so will you.

nonlinear equations

healing isn't a straight line. some days will always be better than others, and sometimes there might be more bad ones than good ones. tomorrow might see you in bed until late afternoon, fighting to do even the simplest things, while the next greets you at sunrise with a cup of coffee and a to-do list that's finished before noon. never let the bad days make you forget that the good ones are waiting for you across the horizon, just as you are waiting for them.

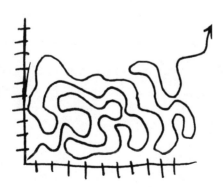

breathe

i am taking in as much life
as my lungs can hold,
and i am learning how to
filter out the toxins

and release the good
back into a world
that so desperately
needs it.

icarus complex

i want to
spread these wings
and climb to the edge
of the atmosphere.

i want to
feel my breath
forced from my lungs
as the air grows thin.

and i want to
hurtle downward
toward the ground
like a shooting star.

just to know i can.

change

it is mornings like this
when i feel most at peace:
sitting at the kitchen table,
coffee mug in hand,

staring out the window
as sunlight breaks
through blooming branches.
like them, i am blooming too.

self-hatred breeds
self-hatred

when you find self-confidence,
they'll try to take it away.
if you feel good about yourself,
then their validation isn't needed,
and they cannot stand being so very
unimportant. they'll try to tear
you down, pick you apart, until the
parts of yourself that you have begun
to love become the same parts you hate.

unapologetic

i will not
fit myself into a box
to meet your expectations.

i will not
twist myself into a knot
to earn your appreciation.

the moon's resistance

the sun tells the moon
that her place is at night
with the stars,
but still she hangs
defiantly
in the midafternoon sky,
refusing
to have her place dictated
by another's expectations.

fact #1

the mirror was never meant to be your enemy.

fact #2

beauty isn't always honest,
and the truth isn't always pretty.

charade

beware of those who want you to believe they
have your best interest at heart

while doing everything in their power to shape
you into their image.

false hero

too many people
want to speak for others
before speaking for
themselves.

too many people
want to make you better
before bettering
themselves.

too many people
will try to save you
when the only one
who needs saving

is themselves.

kill grave

some will do whatever it takes
to convince you they're someone they're not.
they'll speak in half-truths and full lies,
and they'll repeat them as often as it takes
to get you to fall for the trap they've laid.
that's when they'll wrap invisible strings
around your wrists, elbows, ankles, and knees
and make you dance to their old, tired tune.
they'll say everything you want to hear,
break you down just to build you up,
and they'll tell you how you should feel
about it. if you dare question them,
they'll shift the blame and make you
take on every ounce of their guilt.
you might not recognize the warning
signs right away, but when you do,
remember this one thing:
it was not your fault.

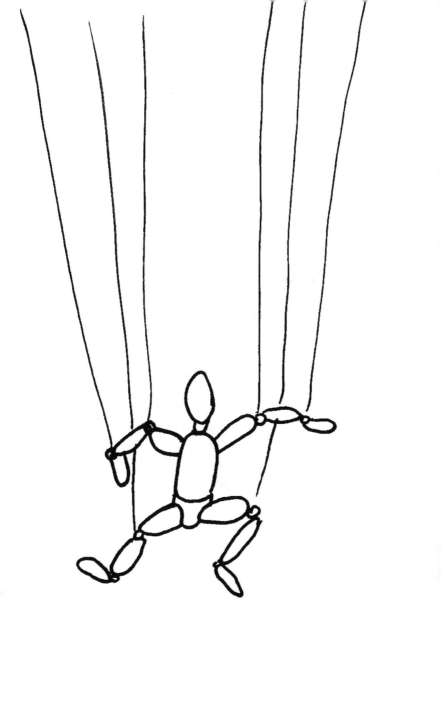

sinful

an image manufactured like
a department store mannequin
dressed in whatever clothes
seem to be trendy this season.
they say envy is the color green,
but it has that in common with greed.
a stolen throne is still stolen even
when it's golden, and the stench
of inauthenticity cannot be hidden
with even the most expensive perfume.

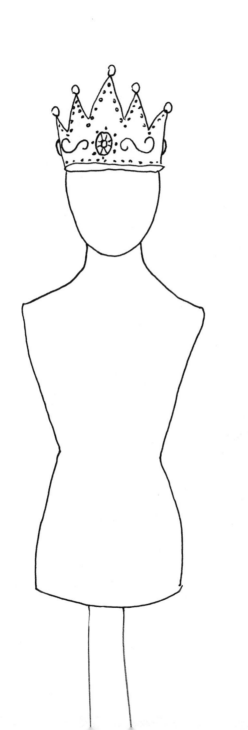

stacked

like a magician
whose first language
is sleight of hand,
they give you the
illusion of control—
pick a card, cut
and shuffle the deck
until you're certain
it's well-hidden, yet
somehow they
always know how
to manipulate their
card back to the top.

less is more

apologize less because you have less to apologize for.

uncaged

it's easy to push people away
to retreat into yourself
to give only the bare minimum.

it's much harder to take that risk
to splay open your chest
to peel each rib back one by one

and bare your heart and soul
to a world that might not handle
them with the care they deserve.

but when you find a person whose
mind complements yours, you'll see
the reward was well worth the risk.

earthquake

society has a way of bending you until you break, no matter how strong you think you are or how hard you try to fight back. it will try to fold you on top of yourself and shape you into something new—something prettier, smaller, less you and more them. but it doesn't realize that by doing so, it's creating a warrior out of you, one strong enough to sink mountains and raise tides. strong enough to reach inside the earth and shake it to its very core. strong enough to leave your mark on what's tried to leave its mark on you.

dawn of a new day

the world may reject you today,

but with time comes understanding.

give it that time, but do not be silent.

let every footstep, every word,

and every breath be an act of revolution.

the world might not be ready for you,

but that doesn't mean you're not ready

to create the tomorrow you deserve.

mythbuster

destroy the idea
that you need to
love yourself
before you can
love someone else
or be loved by them.

self-love
doesn't happen
overnight.

self-love
can be a lifelong
struggle.

self-love
does not dictate
how much love
one deserves,
nor how much
they have to give
to others.

sometimes,
self-love
comes after.

heads & tails

there is comfort in knowing there isn't a single
person who gets the complete picture,

but there is also comfort in knowing that you no
longer have to hide who you really are.

take

sometimes, being a little selfish is the biggest act
of self-love we can give ourselves.

expanse

you are not just a person,
and you don't simply exist.
you are a culmination of
everything you've ever
seen and heard,
loved and hated,
feared and not.

you are the sum
of every action and reaction,
failure and success,
mistake and apology,
every interaction
with another, like
and unlike yourself.

we are all complex beings
with our own stories
and our own perspectives.
and we all deserve
to love and be loved
just the same.

protanomaly

there must be some deeply poetic meaning in being a child of october who cannot see every hue autumn has to offer, and even though some of its beauty is lost on me, i still know it's there.

a few inevitabilities

you can't please everyone.

not everyone will like you.

people will say things behind your back.

you will always have doubters.

these people don't matter.

the sooner you can accept this,

the sooner you can live unapologetically.

the final masquerade

tear off the mask
you've hidden behind
for so long. step out
into the sunlight,
and let it kiss your skin.
run until you haven't
a single breath left,
and take flight.
bathe in moonlight.
paint yourself with starlight.
break free from the world's grip
and become your truest self.
you were always meant to be
your own universe.

space

do what you must to protect your own peace,
and don't let anyone make you feel guilty for doing so.

be

be brave.
be fearless.
let your imagination
run wild.
the world is what you make it,
not what it makes you.

goodbye is a lie
after iain s. thomas

every once in a while, you'll experience a moment where you know your life will never be the same again. there will be no light, no sign that you will be forever altered, just the aching realization that you are now someone new. not completely new. no, you're still you, maybe more you than you've ever been, but different than before. i've spent so many years trying to squeeze myself into places i didn't fit that i had convinced myself there wasn't a place for me, but over the span of five days, that place i had been searching for found me. that place i had been searching for wasn't a place after all but a group of people who accepted me for the person i've finally found the courage to be. *here* is where i belong. *here*, in this moment. *here*, with these people. and goddamn, is it good.

the end

when i'm gone,
i know there's a chance that
no one will pick up this book
to dissect its insides
or sift through the pages of my journal
and marvel at the work i've left behind.
i know there's a chance that
no one will spend class periods
teaching their students these poems
or writing papers about their meanings,
and i know my name may not go down
in history alongside edgar
and emily, langston, and sylvia,
the ones who've inspired me
in some way to put pen to paper.
immortality sounds great,
but it's not what drives me.
i write because there once was a kid
who desperately needed
the words written on these pages.
i write because there still might be someone
who needs them just as badly, and if
what i write can help even one person
accept who they are, then i've already
accomplished everything i set out to do.

acknowledgments

some much-needed thank-yous—

my family, maria, jon, sarah, victoria, rita, terrence, sue, courtney, aj, and the kids, for always being there when i need you and for always believing in me and my writing.

my editor, patty rice, my publisher, kirsty melville, and each and every single person at andrews mcmeel for everything that went into bringing this book to life and for giving me another opportunity to put my words into the world.

the re:ad poetry team of holly stayton, patience randle, rachel cooper, and jamie chaplin for all the hard work and dedication you four put into pushing poetry into as many hands as you possibly can.

trista mateer and caitlyn siehl for helping me work though the identity crisis this book went through about halfway through the writing process, for taking the time to read an early draft of *masquerade* and giving me your honest feedback, and for being two of my favorite people.

alex andrina for being there for me time and time again, especially when i went through my own identity crisis, and for taking the time to read an early draft of this and giving me your honest feedback.

danika stone and summer webb for also reading an early draft of *masquerade* and giving me feedback on it, and for being two of the most genuine and supportive people i have had the honor of knowing.

nikita gill, k.y. robinson, and iain s. thomas, aka the other half of the poetry avengers i have yet to thank, for not only accepting me with open arms but for being constant inspirations to me. may we reassemble soon!

michelle halket of central avenue publishing for bringing the poetry avengers together and for giving versions of the poems "stained glass mirror" and "start→power→shut down" their first home in *[Dis]Connected*.

munise sertel, for the absolutely stunning artwork that graces the cover of this book. when the direction of *masquerade* shifted and it was in need of a face-lift, not only did you deliver but you delivered in spectacular fashion. i cannot thank you enough.

professor dara evans for continuing to be my guiding light, even after graduation, and professor suzanne parker for not only pushing me out of my poetry comfort zone but also for the prompt that inspired the poem "sinful" and the time spent workshopping earlier versions of it.

those in the poetry community who have supported and continue to support me and my work. there's far too many people to name without risk of leaving someone out, but know that i appreciate each and every one of you.

my wife (i'll never get tired of saying that), amanda, whom i owe my entire existence to. thank you for helping me through my constant meltdowns and frequent bouts of imposter syndrome. thank you for helping me work through this book's identity crisis, as well as my own. thank you for your complete understanding, for believing in me, for inspiring me, and for accepting me for who i am. and as always, thank you for being you.

and finally, you, the readers. when an author puts their work out into the world, they never know how it's going to be received. the immense amount of support you've given me and *DROPKICKromance* is something that i truly appreciate with every fiber of my being, and i hope you'll receive *masquerade* just as warmly. thank you for being a part of this journey with me, and i hope you'll come along for the rest of the ride.

— cyrus

about the author

cyrus parker is a pro-wrestler-turned-poet hailing from a small town in new jersey alongside wife and poetess amanda lovelace and their two ragdoll cats, macchiato and rosé. a self-described "big goth kid," cyrus has an affinity for dark eyeshadow, dark clothes, enamel pins, and dropkicking the gender binary.

WEBSITE: http://cyrusparker.com
TWITTER: @cyrusparker
INSTAGRAM: @cyrusparker

index

INDEX

INDEX

masquerade

Andrews McMeel Publishing
a division of Andrews McMeel Universal
1130 Walnut Street, Kansas City, Missouri 64106

www.andrewsmcmeel.com

19 20 21 22 23 BVG 10 9 8 7 6 5 4 3 2 1

ISBN: 978-1-4494-9709-5

Library of Congress Control Number: 2018962703

Cover illustration by Munise Sertel

Editor: Patty Rice
Designer/Art Director: Julie Barnes
Production Editor: Elizabeth A. Garcia
Production Manager: Cliff Koehler

ATTENTION: SCHOOLS AND BUSINESSES
Andrews McMeel books are available at quantity discounts
with bulk purchase for educational, business, or sales promotional use.
For information, please e-mail the Andrews McMeel Publishing
Special Sales Department: specialsales@amuniversal.com.